A BEACON ✺ BIOGRAPHY

Meghan Markle

Kayleen Reusser

PURPLE TOAD
PUBLISHING

PURPLE TOAD
PUBLISHING

Printing   1   2   3   4   5   6   7   8   9

A Beacon Biography

Library of Congress Cataloging-in-Publication Data
Reusser, Kayleen
Meghan Markle / Written by Kayleen Reusser.
     p. cm.
Includes bibliographic references, glossary, and index.
ISBN 9781624694240
1. Meghan Markle. 1981- — Juvenile literature. 2. Royalty — Great Britain — Biography — Juvenile literature. I. Series: A Beacon Biography
 DA591. A45 2019
 941.086092
[B]

Library of Congress Control Number: 2018943921

eBook ISBN: 9781624694233

ABOUT THE AUTHOR: Kayleen Reusser has written more than a dozen books for children and adults. Her interviews with 200 World War II vets have been published in two books: *World War II Legacies: Stories of Northeast Indiana Veterans* and *They Did It for Honor: Stories of American WWII Veterans*. She is also the co-founder of two writing clubs. For more information, visit her web site at www. KayleenReusser.com.

PUBLISHER'S NOTE: This story has not been authorized or endorsed by Meghan Markle.

CONTENTS

Prior to their wedding, Prince Harry and Meghan Markle visited groups like Catalyst Inc. This group works on and celebrates new ideas in science.

Meghan Markle and her fiancé, Harry, strolled through the streets of Nottingham, England, greeting hundreds of people and shaking hands. It was December 1, 2017, and the couple had attended an event to recognize World AIDS Day in England.

Harry's full name is Prince Henry Charles Albert David Mountbatten-Windsor; Harry is his nickname. His grandmother is Queen Elizabeth of England, and his brother, William, is the Prince of Wales. Prince Harry, Prince William, and Queen Elizabeth are members of the British Royal Family.

When the Royal Family travels, they often take part in walkabouts like the one Markle and Harry were doing in Nottingham. Walkabouts allow the public to see the Royal Family face to face.

The walkabout in Nottingham was Markle's first time to greet the people of England since becoming engaged to Harry. The people offered her well wishes, gifts, and flowers. Markle accepted each with smiles of thanks.

Mingling with a large crowd of strangers might seem frightening to some people, but Markle was calm. She had been an actress on TV and in movies for many years. She often met crowds of fans and signed autographs. But greeting strangers while walking beside a member of the British monarchy was different from anything she had ever done.

Before her marriage to Prince Harry, Meghan Markle starred in the hit TV show Suits.

"I had no understanding of what it would be like to be part of the Royal Family," said Markle.[1]

Falling in love with Harry still seemed like something from a fairy tale. She and Harry had met in July 2016 when a friend, Markus Anderson, introduced them. Their first date was at a restaurant in London, England, called The Dean Street Townhouse.

Meghan and Harry soon discovered common interests. Both loved dogs (she owned two, and he had grown up with many in the castles). They liked exercising (he attended a gym while she preferred running outdoors). Most of all, they had a passion for helping people in need.

During the next few months, Markle and Harry kept in touch through phone calls, emails, texts, and some visits. Few people knew of their relationship. Secrecy was vital. As a member of the Royal Family, Harry was closely watched by news media. People who photograph celebrities for the media are called paparazzi. If the paparazzi suspected Harry was dating Markle, they would follow her, too.

Harry had endured media attention all of his life. He knew Markle was a successful actress and had had her photo taken many times by professional photographers. Still, Harry worried that the constant media coverage would make her life difficult. "I tried to warn her," he said, "but both of us were totally surprised by the reaction of the public."[2]

Harry lived in London. He often attended meetings and fund-raisers around the world, all as part of his family's royal duties. Markle spent several months of each year in Toronto, Canada, filming her TV show, *Suits*.

Managing busy schedules could have kept them from spending time together and developing a serious relationship. In fact, the opposite seemed to happen. No matter how busy they were, they found time for each other. They even took a safari in Botswana, Africa. "It was a choice," said Markle during an interview. "Very early on we realized we were going to commit to each other."[3]

Prince Harry at the Invictus Games, 2017. (Invictus is Latin for "unconquered.")

No one knew for sure that Markle and Prince Harry were dating until September 25, 2017. When they sat together to watch a wheelchair tennis event at the Invictus Games in Toronto, people could tell they had a special relationship.

The Invictus Games are part of a multi-sport competition that Harry created for wounded, injured, and ill military people. Harry organized the event after serving as a soldier twice in Afghanistan.

The first Invictus events were held in London in 2014. The next Invictus Games were held in Orlando, Florida, in 2016. By the third set of games in Toronto in 2017, 550 athletes from 16 nations had registered to compete in 11 events.

It was obvious from the way Harry and Markle laughed and chatted while seated next to each other that they knew each other well. People watching them were curious. Had the British prince fallen in love with an American actress?

Harry and Meghan traveled to Ireland together for "Amazing the Space," a project encouraging young people to find ways to bring peace to the world.

A Cinderella Tale

Like characters in the fairy tale *Cinderella*, the lives of Meghan Markle from California and England's Prince Harry could hardly be more different.

Rachel Meghan Markle was born on August 4, 1981. Her parents separated when she was two years old and divorced four years later. Meghan lived with her mother, Doria Ragland, who worked as a yoga instructor and a social worker.

Her father, Thomas Markle, was a camera operator for TV shows in Los Angeles. Meghan's siblings include an older half-sister, Samantha Grant Markle, and an older half-brother, Thomas Markle Jr. The children have the same father.

At an early age, Meghan showed signs of independence. When she was 11 years old, she wrote to a dishwashing soap company: "You should change your ad showing only women washing dishes." Later she told a reporter, "I don't think it's right for kids to grow up thinking that just mom does everything." The soap company understood her point and the commercial was changed.[1]

Meghan attended a private Catholic school in Los Angeles called Immaculate Heart. After school, she often visited the sets for TV shows where her father worked. Meghan chose acting as a career.

At Northwestern University in Evanston, Illinois, Markle majored in theater and international relations. She was the first person from her family to graduate from college.[2]

As an actress, Markle auditioned for many acting roles. In between acting jobs, she worked as a waitress and created calligraphy for clients.

Being a professional actress kept Meghan Markle on the move.

Markle's big acting break came in 2011 when she was cast as Rachel Zane, a paralegal, on *Suits*. She also appeared in romantic movies: *Random Encounters* (2013), *When Sparks Fly* (2014), and *Dater's Handbook* (2017).

Harry's royal life was planned from the minute he took his first breath at St Mary's Hospital in central London on September 15, 1984. His father, Prince Charles, was married to Diana Spencer. Diana's father was an earl, a member of British aristocracy or nobility. Harry's older brother, William, is second in line to be king of

As a preschooler, Prince Harry's smile revealed a somewhat mischievous streak.

England after their father. As of 2018, Harry was sixth in line to the Crown, after William's children.

Harry, like every member of the Royal Family, grew up with bodyguards. They traveled with him at school, and later at Eton College in England. They continue to accompany him everywhere.

With ginger hair and a mischievous grin, Harry seemed to be born with a zest for life. His father taught him how to play polo. Harry likes to ski, and he has had many pets. His mother, Princess Diana, took him to Disneyland and to the beach.

There were sad times, too. Harry's parents divorced when he was 11 years old. Harry and William spent time with both parents, but Harry

Princess Diana dances with actor John Travolta in 1985. As the wife of a prince, Diana attended many gala events that included dancing.

especially loved being with his mother. Diana hugged them often and told them she loved them. When Harry was 12 years old, Diana died in a car accident. Harry struggled for years with grief.

Markle has no royal blood and has had to work to support herself. In comparison, Prince Harry, who is extremely wealthy, will never need to look for a traditional job. He has vacationed around the world. His family owns castles, expensive cars, and land in several countries.

Despite their different backgrounds, Harry and Markle share a strong desire to help people. In 2015 she spoke at International Women's Day for the United Nations. "Having a voice people will listen to comes with a lot of responsibility,"[3] Meghan said during an interview.

In February 2016 she traveled to India and Rwanda for World Vision to learn about the needs of the people living there. To help more people understand that young girls need to have the same opportunities as boys, she wrote many articles for magazines and newspapers.

Prince Harry served in the military for ten years, making two tours in Afghanistan as a soldier for the British army. Afterward, he spent time in the small country of Lesotho, Africa. He made a film about the plight of orphans there to encourage people to help them.

By the time they met, Meghan Markle and Prince Harry had spent much time and effort showing care and concern for other people. Together, could they create a powerful force for doing good around the world?

Having served in the military, Prince Harry values the sacrifices of fellow soldiers.

As part of the British Royal Family, Prince Harry's parents dressed well for every occasion.

Bridging Two Cultures

One night in November 2017, Markle cooked Harry a chicken dinner at his apartment in London. As a bachelor, Harry appreciated the effort she put into the food. Markle loved to cook and often wrote about food and beauty on her blog called The Tig.[1]

For more than a year, Markle and the Prince had dated. They loved each other. Still, it shocked Markle when Harry proposed to her after the meal. "It was an amazing surprise," she said later. "It was so sweet and natural and romantic. He got on one knee. I could barely let him finish proposing."[2]

Prince Harry and Meghan wanted to get married. But there was a problem. Years ago, royal families in Europe arranged marriages— sometimes with strangers—to strengthen their countries' governments. In recent years, royalty married for love with people from other titled families (for example, Diana's father was an earl). Markle was not a member of a royal family. Her father was white. Her mother was black. If Markle married Prince Harry, she would not only be the first American to join the British Royal Family, she would be the first biracial member.

Markle is proud of her mixed-race heritage. But as a child she was sometimes confused. In seventh grade she was told to check a box on a form at school indicating her ethnicity: white, black, Hispanic, or Asian. Years later, she told a reporter, "There I was with my curly hair, freckled face, pale skin and mixed race. I looked at the boxes, not knowing what to do. You could only choose one, but that would be to choose one parent over the other—and one half of myself over the other. My teacher told me to check the box for Caucasian. 'Because that's how you look, Meghan,' she said."

Markle put down her pen. "Not as an act of defiance," she explained, "but rather a symptom of my confusion. I couldn't picture the sadness my mother would feel if she were to find out. So, I didn't tick a box."[3]

Meghan Markle was not royalty, and she was biracial, but there was an even bigger reason she might not be able to marry Harry. In 2011, she had married American producer Trevor Engelson. They divorced two years later.

Queen Elizabeth is head of the Church of England. She has the power to decide whom her family can marry. In the past, Queen Elizabeth did not allow members of the Royal Family, including her sister, to marry people who were divorced. It was against the rules set up long ago for the British monarchy.

Today, the rules have changed. The Queen understands that people do not always stay happily married. After meeting Markle and seeing the love between her and Harry, the Queen gave

Elizabeth was crowned Queen in 1953.

St. George's Chapel seats approximately 800 people for services.

permission for them to marry.

Markle and Harry selected the date of May 19, 2018, for their wedding. It would be held at St. George's Chapel at Windsor Castle. Windsor Castle, about an hour's drive west of London, is one of Queen Elizabeth's many grand homes.

Marrying into the British Royal Family would bring big changes for Markle. She had to give up her successful acting career and move from Canada to London. No member of the Royal Family is allowed to act on TV or in movies. She would never sign another autograph. She had to close down all of her social media sites, including her blog. Staff people representing the Royal Family would post for her on social media.

Like many married women, Markle's name would change. She would be called Her Royal Highness (HRH) Meghan, and Meghan, Duchess of Sussex. Before the wedding, she would complete the process of becoming a British citizen and be baptized into the Church of England.

For the rest of her life Markle would have security people with her in public. She would never go shopping alone, vote, or be active in politics. She could not wear jeans or take selfies.[4]

A change of name, religion, country, and career—what more was in store for Meghan Markle in her role as a member of England's Royal Family?

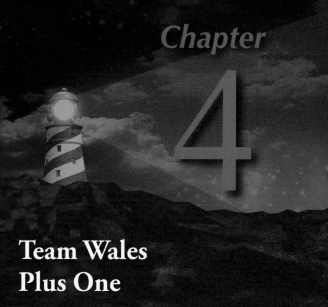

As Prince Harry's fiancée, Meghan Markle was eager to try new experiences, such as putting on a parachute like a British soldier.

Team Wales Plus One

From the time Meghan accepted Harry's wedding proposal, she showed support for the British Royal Family. At interviews with reporters, she spoke easily about her relationship with Harry. She greeted thousands of people during Harry's and her trip throughout the British Isles in the spring 2018.

Much of Markle's confidence comes from her experience as an actress. She had given dozens of interviews to reporters. Early in her career, she worked to build her self-esteem. She refused to read anything written about her in newspapers, magazines, or online. "The people who are close to me anchor me in knowing who I am," she said. "The rest is noise."[1]

As a member of one of the world's most famous families, Markle would use her confidence at many political events and fund-raisers. She would also visit hospitals and schools and other places that helped people.

Philanthropy work was exciting to Markle. "My mother brought me up to be a 'global citizen', " she said. "My parents came from little so they made a choice to give a lot: buying turkeys for homeless shelters at Thanksgiving, delivering meals to people in hospices, giving spare change to those asking for it. It's what I grew up seeing, so it's what I grew up being: a young adult with a social consciousness to do what I could and speak up when I knew something was wrong."[2]

At age 13, Markle learned a valuable lesson about helping people. She had volunteered to work in a soup kitchen on Skid Row in Los Angeles. Even though she was with a group of volunteers, she felt overwhelmed. "The first day I felt really scared," she said. "I was young, and it was rough and raw down there."

Then one of her mentors said something Markle never forgot: "Life is about putting others' needs above your own fears."

Those words made a big impact on Markle's life. Today, she offers advice to young people who want to volunteer: "Make sure you are safe and never, ever put yourself in a compromising situation. Remember that someone needs us. Your act of giving and helping and doing can truly become an act of grace once you get out of your head."[3]

Meghan supported the United Service Organizations (USO), which provides entertainment for the American military.

Princess Diana attended dozens of events each year. Her selflessness has been encouraging to Harry and to Meghan.

Markle knew she would need every bit of poise she could muster to be a contributing member of the British Royal Family. She recalled how Harry's mother, Princess Diana, had found the pressures of living in the public eye especially difficult.

From the minute she had become engaged to Prince Charles in 1981, Diana was followed day and night by photographers and reporters. They hounded her with a barrage of questions, wanting to know every detail of her life. Over time, Diana became depressed. She suffered from bulimia (an eating disorder) and tried to commit suicide.

But Diana was a good mother. She wanted her sons to care about people outside of the Palace. She took them to homeless shelters and

The British people loved Princess Diana's willingness to accept all people.

places where people who suffered from AIDS were cared for. In the 1980s, people believed they would get AIDS (acquired immunodeficiency syndrome) by touching someone with the virus. When doctors told Diana that was not true, she held hands with people who had AIDS. By doing so, she lessened people's fear of the disease.

Diana's example had a lasting effect on her sons. At a service in 2007 to honor Diana, ten years after her death, Harry said, "She will always be remembered for her amazing public work. She was quite simply the best mother in the world. She made us and so many other people happy."[4]

Like his mother, Harry struggled for years with the paparazzi. They took photos of him drinking under age and getting into other trouble. Harry apologized for his poor behavior and admitted he sometimes wished he weren't a prince. "I wanted out, but then decided to stay in and work out a role for myself," he said.[5]

One thing that helped Harry was helping others. In January 2005 he and William, who called themselves Team Wales, packed supplies for tsunami victims for the Red Cross. They also set up the Charitable Foundation of Prince William and Prince Harry. This organization provides grants to help wounded servicemen and young people in need.

As Harry's wife, Meghan would join Team Wales, and continue to help make a difference.

Prince Harry (right) and Prince William (left) formed Team Wales to help people in need. One event was a charity polo match.

Once they were married, Meghan and Harry moved in to Kensington Palace in London.

Living as a Princess

Meghan Markle has a life most people can only dream of. She will meet important people around the world. She will never worry about not having enough food to eat or clothes to wear or whether she can afford a vacation. Her children will have the best schools, medical care, and opportunities.

But not everything has been smooth for Markle. As soon as people knew that she and Harry were dating, Markle became one of the most recognized celebrities in the world. Everything she did—from what she ate to what kind of shoes she wore—was photographed and discussed through regular and social media.

When Harry was asked how he coped with strangers wanting to know so many details about his life, he said, "We know we have certain responsibilities, but within our private life, we want to be as normal as possible. It's hard because to a certain [extent] we will never be normal."[1]

By marrying Harry, Markle knew she would be living her life in a fish bowl. "I don't see it as giving anything up," she told the BBC. "I just see it as a change."[2]

In November 2016, some reporters wrote nasty stories about Markle, falsely claiming she grew up in a "gangster" neighborhood of Los Angeles. They made her childhood sound more dangerous than it was.[3]

Harry was accustomed to negative press, and he refused to allow the paparazzi to talk about Markle so rudely. He issued a statement condemning their actions and asked them to leave her alone.[4] Harry probably wanted his fiancée to avoid the same pressures the media had placed on his mother twenty years earlier.

The media agreed to back off a little. The stage was set to focus at last on the wedding.

The wedding at St. George's Chapel on May 19, 2018, took months of preparation. Thousands attended, and nearly a billion people around the world watched on TV and online. As Markle walked down the aisle, her white silk gown flowed behind her. Her veil was covered with embroidered flowers from the 53 countries under England's rule. Meghan's home state of California was also represented with a poppy, its state flower. Holding the veil in place was a diamond-studded tiara that had belonged to Harry's great-grandmother, Queen Mary.

Typically, a bride holds her father's arm during the march, but Meghan's father was ill and unable to attend. In his place Meghan asked her future father-in-law, Prince Charles, to escort her. Prince Charles was happy to stand in. Behind the procession of ten pageboys and bridesmaids, he walked her to the altar, where a smiling Harry waited. Clearly, Prince Charles and the rest of the Royal Palace had accepted Meghan as a true daughter of the British monarchy.

Thousands of people had been invited to the wedding. These included members of the royal family, schoolchildren, military veterans, people associated with Harry's charities, and celebrities such

During the wedding of Prince Harry and Meghan Markle, millions of people around the world watched the couple exchange vows via television and online media.

as actor George Clooney, singer Sir Elton John, tennis star Serena Williams, and Oprah Winfrey. Hundreds of other people stood along the three-mile road leading to the chapel. Queen Elizabeth looked regal in her green and violet suit, while Meghan's mother, looking proud as Megan and Harry took their vows, drew admiring glances.

The multicultural ceremony was conducted by the Reverend Michael Curry, an African American, who quoted Martin Luther King Jr. when he said, "We must discover the redemptive power of love." The music combined a traditional hymn ("Guide Me, O Thou Great Redeemer") with the rock ballad "Stand by Me." Sheku Kanneh-Mason, aged 19, played a lovely cello solo.

After the wedding, Meghan and Harry rode away from Windsor Castle in an open carriage pulled by four white horses. With this fairy-tale ending, it was hard to imagine how it could get any better for the latest Royal Couple.

Then on October 15, 2018, Meghan announced she was expecting their first child. Not a bad way to end a story, or to start a new one.

1981   Meghan Markle is born August 4 in Los Angeles, California.

1983   Meghan's mother separates from her father. Meghan lives with her mother.

1984   Prince Harry is born on September 15.

1987   Markle's parents divorce.

1992   Markle writes to Procter and Gamble to ask them to change their dish soap advertisement.

1997   Harry's mother, Princess Diana, dies in a car crash.

1999   Markle graduates from Immaculate Heart High School.

2003   She graduates from Northwestern University in Chicago with majors in international relations and theater.

2011   Markle lands the role of Rachel Zane on the Canadian legal drama *Suits*. She marries American producer Trevor Engelson.

2013   Markle and Engelson divorce. She stars in the romantic movie *Random Encounters*.

2014   Markle stars in the romantic movie *When Sparks Fly*.

2015   Markle speaks at International Women's Day for the United Nations.

2016   She stars in the romantic movie *Dater's Handbook*. She meets Prince Harry in London. She travels to India and Rwanda for World Vision.

2017   Prince Harry proposes; Markle accepts and resigns from *Suits*.

2018   Markle moves to London, becomes a British citizen, and joins the Church of England. She marries Prince Harry on May 19. Her cookbook, *Together: Our Community Cookbook*, is released. Sales will benefit the Hubb Community Kitchen in London. In October, she and Harry announce that they are expecting their first child in Spring 2019. They plan to move into a 21-room apartment in Kensington Palace, next door to William and Kate.

Chapter 1

1. Mishal Husain, *Meghan Markle and Prince Harry's First TV Interview in Full—Video, The Guardian,* November 27, 2017.
2. Ibid.
3. Ibid.

Chapter 2

1. Mark Matousek, "Resurfaced Video Shows a Young Meghan Markle Asking Proctor & Gamble to Change a Commercial with Sexist Overtones," *BusinessInsider.com,* December 1, 2017.
2. "Meghan's Rise to Royalty," *New York Post,* November 28, 2017.
3. Mishal Husain, *Meghan Markle and Prince Harry's First TV Interview in Full—Video, The Guardian.* November 27, 2017.

Chapter 3

1. Tara John, "Meet Meghan Markle, Prince Harry's Fiancée and Britain's Newest Royal-To-Be," *Time.com,* November 27, 2017.
2. Katie Reilly, "Prince Harry and Meghan Markle Share Their Engagement Story and How They First Met," *Time.com,* November 27, 2017.
3. "American Princess: A New Role for the 'Calif. Girl' Who Captured Harry's Heart," *The New York Post,* November 28, 2017.
4. Erica Gonzales, "Meghan Markle and Prince Harry Just Visited a Castle Together," *Harpersbazaar.com,* January 19, 2018.

Chapter 4

1. Olivia Blair, "8 Things We Learned from Meghan Markle's Latest Interview," *HarpersBazaar.com,* September 5, 2017.
2. Tara John, "Meet Meghan Markle, Prince Harry's Fiancée and Britain's Newest Royal-To-Be," *Time.com,* November 27, 2017.
3. "Meghan: I Was So Scared Helping in LA Soup Kitchen When I Was 13," *Daily Mail* (London, England), January 1, 2018.
4. Katie Nicholl, *William and Harry: Behind the Palace Walls* (New York: Weinstein Books, 2010), p. 223.
5. Ashitha Nagesh, "Prince Harry Considered Quitting Royal Family to Live Life as a Commoner," *Metro UK,* June 25, 2017.

Chapter 5

1. Katie Nicholl, *William and Harry: Behind the Palace Walls* (New York: Weinstein Books, 2010), p. 218.
2. Michelle Tauber, "Prince Harry & Meghan Markle Engaged!" *People,* December 11, 2017.
3. Louise Berwick, "Harry to Marry into Gangster Royalty? New Love 'From Crime-Ridden Neighbourhood,' " *Daily Star,* November 3, 2016.
4. Josh Duboff, "After Asking for Privacy, Prince Harry and Meghan Markle Remain under the Spotlight", *Vanity Fair,* November 10, 2016.

Books

Carroll, Leslie. *The Love Story of Meghan Markle and Prince Harry.* New York: William Morrow, 2018.

Morton, Andrew. *Meghan: A Hollywood Princess.* New York: Grand Central Publishing, 2018.

Sadat, Halima. *Harry and Meghan: A Royal Engagement.* London: Pavilion, 2018.

Works Consulted

Andersen, Christopher. *After Diana: William, Harry, Charles, and the Royal House of Windsor.* New York: Hyperion, 2007.

Blair, Olivia. "Yes, She Really Is Madly in Love with Prince Harry." *Harpers Bazaar,* September 5, 2017.

Boone, Mary. *Royal Romance: The Love Story of William and Kate.* Chicago: Triumph Books, 2011.

Bullen, Annie. *William: Duke of Cambridge.* London: Pitkin Publishing, 2012.

Husain, Mishal. *Meghan Markle and Prince Harry's First TV Interview in Full—Video, The Guardian,* November 27, 2017.

Levin, Angela. "Prince of Hearts." *Newsweek Global.* June 30, 2017, Vol. 168, Issue 24, pp. 32–41.

Nicholl, Katie. *The Making of a Royal Romance.* New York: Weinstein Books, 2010.

Nicholl, Katie. *William and Harry: Behind the Palace Walls.* NewYork: Weinstein Books, 2010.

Puente, Maria. " 'Loved up' Harry, Meghan Give Fans a Treat." *USA Today,* January 10, 2018.

Reilly, Katie. "Prince Harry and Meghan Markle Share Their Engagement Story and How They First Met." *Time.com,* November 27, 2017, p. 40.

The Royals: Their Lives, Loves and Secrets. New York: Time Home Entertainment, 2007.

Seward, Ingrid. *William & Harry.* New York: Arcade, 2003.

Tauber, Michelle. "Meghan Markle: Her Road to Royalty." *People.com,* December 18, 2017, Vol. 88 Issue 25, pp. 38–42.

Tauber, Michelle. "Prince Harry & Meghan Markle Engaged!" *People.com,* December 11, 2017, Vol. 88 Issue 24, pp. 50–56.

On the Internet

British Royal Family website: https://www.royal.uk/.

aristocracy (ayr-uh-STOK-ruh-see)—The group of people who hold exceptional rank and privileges; a member of the governing body or upper class usually belonging to the nobility.

audition (aw-DIH-shun)—A tryout for a performance.

barrage (buh-RAHJ)—A heavy and continuous firing of questions.

biracial (by-RAY-shul)—Having a biological mother from one race and a biological father from another.

calligraphy (kuh-LIH-gruh-fee)—Fancy penmanship.

compromising (KOM-pruh-mahy-zing)—Describing a shameful or dangerous situation.

defiance (dee-FY-unts)—Fighting against authority.

hospice (HOS-pis)—A place or a plan for the terminally ill that focuses on making their last days comfortable.

international (in-ter-NASH-uh-nul)—Involving two or more nations.

intrusive (in-TROO-siv)—Forcefully or wrongfully present.

mingle (MING-ul)—To mix with other people.

monarchy (MAH-nar-kee)—A government ruled by a single person; a country that has such a government.

nobility (noh-BIL-ih-tee)—High society in a country.

paparazzi (pah-puh-RAHT-see)—Freelance photographers, especially those who sell candid pictures of celebrities to the media.

paralegal (par-uh-LEE-gul)—Attorney's assistant trained to perform certain legal tasks.

philanthropy (fil-AN-thruh-pee)—Acts or gifts that are done to help people or groups in need.

poise (POYZ)—An easy, gracious, confident manner.

polo (POH-loh)—A game played on horseback between two teams of four players who try to score points by driving a wooden ball into the opponents' goal using a long-handled mallet.

pomp (POMP)—Splendor; magnificence.

safari (suh-FAR-ee)—A journey for hunting or exploration, usually in Africa.

tsunami (soo-NAH-mee)—An unusually large sea wave produced by undersea earth movements.

INDEX